GREAT AFRICAN-AMERICAN WOMEN

Rosa Parks

Erinn Banting

WEIGL PUBLISHERS INC.

Published by Weigl Publishers Inc.
350 5th Avenue, Suite 3304, PMB 6G
New York, NY USA 10118-0069
Web site: www.weigl.com

All of the Internet URLs given in the book were valid at the time of publication. However, due to the dynamic nature of the Internet, some addresses may have changed, or sites may have ceased to exist since publication. While the author and publisher regret any inconvenience this may cause readers, no responsibility for any such changes can be accepted by either the author or the publisher.

Library of Congress Cataloging-in-Publication Data

Banting, Erinn.
  Rosa Parks / Erinn Banting.
    p. cm. -- (Great African American women)
  Includes index.
  ISBN 1-59036-336-1 (hard cover : alk. paper) --
ISBN 1-59036-342-6 (soft cover : alk. paper)
  1. Parks, Rosa, 1913---Juvenile literature. 2. African American women--Alabama--Montgomery--Biography--Juvenile literature. 3. African Americans--Alabama--Montgomery--Biography--Juvenile literature. 4. Civil rights workers--Alabama--Montgomery--Biography--Juvenile literature. 5. African Americans--Civil rights--Alabama--Montgomery--History--20th century--Juvenile literature. 6. Segregation in transportation--Alabama--Montgomery--History--20th century--Juvenile literature. 7. Montgomery (Ala.)--Race relations--Juvenile literature. 8. Montgomery (Ala.)--Biography--Juvenile literature. I. Title. II. Series.
  F334.M753P38236 2005
  323'.092--dc22
  2004029960

Printed and bound in the United States of America
1 2 3 4 5 6 7 8 9 0   09 08 07 06 05

Project Coordinator Janice L. Redlin
Copy Editor Heather C. Hudak
Design Terry Paulhus **Layout** Kathryn Livingstone
Photo Research Kim Winiski and Annalise Bekkering

Photograph Credits
Every reasonable effort has been made to trace ownership and to obtain permission to reprint copyright material. The publishers would be pleased to have any errors or omissions brought to their attention so that they may be corrected in subsequent printings.

Cover: Rosa Parks has become an important symbol in the United States' civil rights movement.

Cover: Getty Images/William Philpott (front); Getty Images/Larry Downing (back); **Corbis:** 22B; **Getty Images:** pages 1 (Paul Schutzer/Time & Life Pictures), 3 (William Philpott), 5 (Taro Yamasaki/Time & Life Pictures), 6T (Don Cravens/Time & Life Pictures), 6B (Kean Collection/Hulton Archive), 7TL (National Archive/Newsmakers), 7BL (Hans Neleman/The Image Bank), 8 (MPI/Hulton Archive), 9T (Don Cravens/Time & Life Pictures), 9B (Taro Yamasaki/Time & Life Pictures), 10 (Microzoa/The Image Bank), 11 (Robert W. Kelley/Time & Life Pictures), 12 (Steve Allen/Brand X Pictures), 13 (Hisham F. Ibrahim/Photodisc Red), 14 (Don Cravens/Time & Life Pictures), 15L (Paul Schutzer/Time & Life Pictures), 15R (Consolidated News Pictures), 16 (Bob Parent/Hulton Archive), 17 (Time & Life Pictures/DMI), 18 (Richard Ellis), 19T (Bill Greenblatt), 19B (William Philpott), 20 (Bill Pierce/Time & Life Pictures), 21BL (Paul J. Richards/AFP), 21TR (Keystone/Hulton Archive), 21BR (Hrvoje Polan), 22T (Siede Preis/Photodisc Green), 22M (Photodisc Blue); **Lenox and Tilden Foundations:** page 4; **Gregg Muller:** page 21MR; **Photos.com:** pages 7R.

Rosa Parks

CONTENTS

Great African-American Women

Who is Rosa Parks?

Rosa Parks is known worldwide as the "Mother of the **Civil Rights Movement**." Rosa grew up in the southern United States, where African Americans faced **racism**, violence, and **discrimination**. She helped African Americans fight for their **rights**.

From a young age, Rosa believed in equal rights for all people. She fought for equal rights as an **activist**, writer, and speaker. Rosa's work has made a difference to African Americans. Her struggles have helped African Americans win the right to vote and attend school. When Rosa writes and speaks, she encourages people to treat all cultures equally and with respect. Many people think Rosa is a hero as her life and work have **inspired** them.

Whatever my individual desires were to be free, I was not alone. There were many others who felt the same way.

Growing Up in the South

Rosa was born on February 4, 1913, in Tuskegee, Alabama. Her mother, Leona McCauley, was a teacher. Her father, James McCauley, was a carpenter. Life for Rosa's family was very difficult. Her father traveled around the country to find work. He was gone for months and years at a time. After Rosa's brother, Sylvester, was born, the family moved to Pine Level, Alabama.

Rosa's grandparents owned a farm in Pine Level. Few African Americans owned land in the South at that time. Rosa helped her grandparents work on the farm. Her grandparents were former **slaves**. Rosa's grandparents were very proud not to work for other people. They taught Rosa to stand up for her rights. Rosa's grandparents also believed school was very important.

Almost 75 percent of the 2.5 million slaves in the United States helped produce cotton.

ALABAMA Tidbits

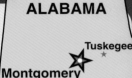

ALABAMA

Tuskegee

Montgomery

FLAG	SEAL	BIRD	TREE	FLOWER
		Yellowhammer	Southern longleaf pine	Camellia

The first night airplane flight was made at Orville Wright's flying school near Montgomery.

Tuskegee University was founded in 1881 to train African-American teachers. It is now a private university.

Alabama is the only state that contains all of the necessary resources to make iron and steel.

Alabama workers built the first rocket designed to take humans to the moon.

Cotton was Alabama's main crop in the 1800s. After 1915, the boll weevil—a beetle that infests cotton plants—caused much damage to the cotton crops. Farmers began raising livestock and crops other than cotton.

In 1902, Dr. Luther Leonidas Hill performed the first open-heart surgery in the western hemisphere in Alabama. He repaired a stab wound in a young boy's heart.

Think about it!

How might living in the state of Alabama have influenced Rosa? Research your state's sites and symbols, and write about how they might have influenced you and your family.

The Importance of Education

As a child, Rosa was a hard worker both in school and on the farm. African Americans had a shorter school year than other children, so African Americans could work in the fields during the harvest season. Rosa and her family thought all children should receive the same amount of education.

Cotton grew well in the southern United States, but it was difficult to gather and process. Slaves were used to plant and harvest the cotton.

When Rosa grew up, most public places, including schools, were segregated. There were separate places for African Americans to sit on buses and trains, theaters, churches, and parks.

In the 1920s to 1950s in the United States, African Americans were not allowed to drink from the same water fountains as people of European ancestry. African Americans who broke these rules were jailed or beaten.

When Rosa was 11 years old, she began attending the Montgomery Industrial School. The teachers at this school did not believe in **segregation**. Rosa was forced to leave school at 16 years of age to care for her sick grandmother. In 1932, Rosa married Raymond Parks, a barber from Montgomery. Raymond believed in education for African Americans. He helped Rosa earn her high school diploma. Rosa completed high school in 1933.

Rosa believes in education and has visited many classrooms to speak to students about her life.

Education as a Tool

Rosa had many **influential** teachers. She learned English, mathematics, geography, and science. African-American children were taught only a few subjects. The teachers seldom had books or supplies. Still, the classes Rosa took helped her teach other African Americans when she was older.

One of Rosa's teachers, Alice L. White, taught Rosa to believe in herself. Miss White encouraged Rosa to be proud of her life. Miss White also instructed Rosa to fight for her beliefs. Later in life, these teachings helped Rosa to fight for the rights of African Americans.

Through Rosa's education, she developed a belief that being an active citizen would improve the world. The civil rights movement was one way for Rosa to practice what she had learned.

Active Citizenship

An active citizen plays a role in building a stronger society. An active citizen is a member of society who participates in society. That participation leads to sharing the benefits that society has to offer.

Natural Rights
- ☑ belong to people by virtue of their human nature. In the United States, these are the rights to life, liberty, and the pursuit of happiness.

Civil Rights
- ☑ are stated in laws or a constitution. The right to vote and hold office as an elected **representative** are civil rights.

Responsiblities
- ☑ voting
- ☑ paying taxes
- ☑ military service
- ☑ obeying laws
- ☑ supporting oneself and one's family

African-American students were educated separately from other children until 1954, when the Supreme Court ruled this practice as illegal.

How People Change Laws

African-American activists worked to change unfair laws during the 1950s and 1960s. Rosa decided to change the laws after an uncomfortable bus ride one day. She often rode the Montgomery, Alabama, bus on her way home from work. Rosa was tired of being segregated. On December 1, 1955, the bus driver asked Rosa to give up her seat for a passenger of European ancestry. Rosa refused, even though she knew she would be arrested.

The next day, African Americans in Montgomery joined together in a **boycott**. They refused to use public buses for 381 days. Over time, the bus line shut down. It did not make enough money without these riders.

Rosa's actions and the boycott that followed led to a court case that was taken to the Supreme Court. By December 1956, the Supreme Court ordered that segregation on Montgomery buses was **unconstitutional**. Rosa's efforts succeeded in changing the law.

The Capitol houses the meeting chambers for the House of Representatives and the Senate. These two groups play key roles in creating the laws of the United States.

To pass a law, the Government of the United States must follow a series of steps. These steps can involve many people. Rosa worked with some of these people to ensure changes to the treatment of African Americans.

Bill

A bill is an idea for a law. Members of **Congress** from the upper house, representatives from the **Senate**, and the **House of Representatives**, or the lower house, can introduce a bill.

Sponsor

The person who introduces the bill is called its sponsor.

Second Reading

Members discuss whether the bill should become a law. They also suggest changes to the bill.

Committee

A committee reviews each bill. If the committee decides the law should not be passed, it is tabled, or set aside. If the bill is accepted, it will have a second reading.

Review

One house must approve a bill. The bill is sent to the other house for approval. The second house follows the same process the first house did.

Passed

If the bill is passed, the speaker of the house and the vice president sign the bill. The bill is sent to the president. When the president signs the bill, it becomes a law.

Montgomery, Alabama, Highlights

Montgomery is the **capital** of Alabama. Many important members of the civil rights movement lived and worked in Montgomery. The city is known as the birthplace of the civil rights movement. People from around the world visit the Rosa Parks Library and Museum. There, they learn about the challenges African Americans faced.

African Americans in Montgomery started riding the bus again when the United States made segregation illegal.

montgomery
Quick Facts

Nickname: the Heart and Soul of the South

Claims to Fame: the Civil Rights Memorial

The Civil Rights Memorial is a monument. It is dedicated to the people who died fighting for civil rights for African Americans. The memorial lists the names of these people.

Martin Luther King, Junior, was a preacher who worked at the Dexter Avenue Baptist Church in Montgomery. He helped Rosa organize the boycott of the Montgomery buses. King became one of the greatest heroes of the civil rights movement.

Martin Luther King, Jr., was awarded the Nobel Peace Prize in 1964. The award was given in recognition of his role in the American civil rights movement.

Overcoming Obstacles

Rosa's struggles with racism were part of a larger situation. The civil rights movement developed during the 1950s and continued into the 1960s. During this time, African Americans who spoke out for their rights were jailed, beaten, and some people lost their lives. Rosa was arrested when she refused to give up her seat on the bus. The Supreme Court case that followed was one step toward overcoming racism.

Demonstrations, marches, and riots in the United States were part of the civil rights movement. Some people even died for the cause.

Many people did not like Rosa's activism. People spoke out against her work in this area. She lost jobs because her employers did not agree with her beliefs. She was even forced to move to a new home. People said they might hurt Rosa and her family if she did not move.

Still, Rosa fought for her beliefs. She continues to work for equality for all people.

Rosa's struggles have been acknowledged by prominent African Americans, including Oprah Winfrey.

Special Achievements

Rosa helped begin the civil rights movement in the United States. She was one of many brave African Americans who spoke out for equal rights. In 1987, Rosa won the Roger Joseph Prize. This award is given to a person who has made a difference in the world. Rosa donated the $10,000 award to the Rosa and Raymond Parks Institute for Self Development. This institute offers career training for young people, with a focus on education and motivation.

Rosa did not attend **college**. Still, she has received more than forty **honorary degrees**. Rosa has also received many other awards and honors. She received the Presidential Medal of Freedom in 1996 and the Congressional Gold Medal in 1999. These are the highest awards given to people in the United States who have made the country a better place to live.

Rosa received the Congressional Gold Medal in the Capitol. The event was attended by lawmakers and members of the civil rights community.

In 2000, a stretch of highway in Missouri was unveiled with the name Rosa Parks Highway.

Museums, libraries, and schools are just some of the places named after Rosa. Many museums also have Rosa Parks' displays. The Smithsonian Institution in Washington, DC, has a sculpture of Rosa. The Smithsonian is one of the largest museums and research and education centers in the world.

Important Times for Rosa

Rosa has overcome many challenges. She is proud of her achievements. Rosa has been honored for her part in the civil rights movement.

In 1943, Rosa became the secretary of Montgomery's National Association for the Advancement of Colored People (NAACP). By 1955, Rosa had formed the Montgomery Improvement Association with Martin Luther King, Jr., and others after she refused to give up her seat on the bus.

Rosa has received many awards. In 1980, she received the Martin Luther King Junior Non-Violent Peace Prize. In 1984, Rosa received the Eleanor Roosevelt Women of Courage Award. She also received the first International Freedom Conductor Award by the National Underground Railroad Freedom Center in 1988.

In 1988, Rosa shared the stage with Reverend Jesse Jackson at the Democratic National Convention. Both are recognized as leaders in the civil rights movement.

Time Line

DECADE	ROSA PARKS	WORLD EVENTS
1910s	Rosa is born February 4, 1913, in Tuskegee, Alabama.	In 1913, Henry Ford develops the first moving assembly line for producing cars.
1930s	In 1932, Rosa marries Raymond Parks.	Construction begins on the Golden Gate Bridge in San Francisco in 1932.
1950s	In 1955, Rosa refuses to give up her seat on a bus. She is arrested.	The board game *Scrabble* is introduced in 1955.
1980s	Rosa helps create the Rosa and Raymond Parks Institute for Self Development in 1987.	A large earthquake hits Los Angeles, California, in 1987.
1990s	In 1996, Rosa is awarded the Presidential Medal of Freedom. In 1999, Rosa receives the Congressional Gold Medal.	In 1999, Nelson Mandela steps down from his position as president of South Africa.

Making a Bill

Are there any changes you would like to make in your home? For example, you may wish to change your chores. In this activity, you can learn how to present your own bill to make the changes you want.

1. Decide on an idea for your bill. Name the bill. For example: Request for a Later Bedtime.

2. Write the bill in three sections. 1) Explain your idea. 2) Explain why the change will be an improvement. 3) Explain how the change will take place.

3. Choose two people to represent the House of Representatives and the Senate. Choose one of these people to be your sponsor.

4. Sit down with your sponsor and discuss the bill. If your sponsor disagrees with parts of it, suggest changes. When you both agree, take it to the other representative.

5. Discuss any changes the other representative would like to make. If the representative disagrees with any part of the bill, invite the representative to discuss changes.

6. Once you reach an agreement, sign the new bill. This makes the change official.

Materials needed:

paper
pens

Now you understand how to go about making changes in your life.

Further Research

Further Reading

Davis, Kenneth C. *Don't Know Much About Rosa Parks*.
Langhorne, PA: Harper Trophy, 2005.

Kudlinski, Kathleen. *Rosa Parks*. New York, NY:
Aladdin, 2001.

Web Sites

To learn more about Rosa's life and career,
log on to these sites.

Academy of Achievement

www.achievement.org/autodoc/
page/par0bio-1

Rosa and Raymond Parks
Institute for Self Development

www.rosaparks.org

Rosa Parks Library and Museum

montgomery.troy.edu/museum

Words to Know

activist: a person who is engaged in political activity

boycott: to refuse to use a product or service in order to change the way that product or service is delivered

capital: the head city in a state

civil rights movement: the struggle of African Americans to gain equal rights

college: a school of higher learning that people attend after high school

Congress: the law-making body of the United States government

discrimination: the act of treating someone differently because of their culture

honorary degrees: degrees given to someone because of the important things that person has achieved

House of Representatives: the lower law-making house of the United States Congress

influential: having or exercising power

inspired: to have an idea, feeling, or reason to do something

racism: dislike of a person because of his or her culture

representative: a person who acts for others

rights: powers granted by an agreement or law

segregation: the practice of having public places that are separated for people of different cultures

Senate: the upper law-making house of the United States Congress

slaves: people who are forced to work without pay

unconstitutional: illegal according to the Constitution

Index